D1171371

The Broadstone Books | Thomas Merton Series

EXPLORING THE LIFE AND WORK OF
THOMAS MERTON
IN THE CONTEXT AND CULTURE OF HIS TIME
AND OURS

PREVIOUS TITLES IN THE SERIES

On the Banks of Monks Pond:
The Thomas Merton / Jonathan Greene Correspondence

Pax Intrantibus:
A Meditation on the Poetry of Thomas Merton
Frederick Smock

A MEETING OF ANGELS

*The Correspondence of Thomas Merton
with Edward Deming & Faith Andrews*

Edited and introduced by
Paul M. Pearson

With photographs of Pleasant Hill by
Thomas Merton

BROADSTONE BOOKS

ISBN 978-0-9721144-9-3

LCCN 2008933126

THE LETTERS AND PHOTOGRAPHS OF THOMAS MERTON
COPYRIGHT © 2008 BY THE MERTON LEGACY TRUST

THE LETTERS OF EDWARD DEMING AND FAITH ANDREWS
COPYRIGHT © 2008 BY ANN E. KANE

TEXT COPYRIGHT © 2008 BY PAUL M. PEARSON

PHOTOGRAPH OF THOMAS MERTON BY JAMES LAUGHLIN
COURTESY OF THE ESTATE OF JAMES LAUGHLIN AND
THE NEW DIRECTIONS OWNERSHIP TRUST

PHOTOGRAPH OF EDWARD DEMING AND FAITH ANDREWS
COURTESY OF ANN E. KANE

CAPTIONS FOR THE MERTON PHOTOGRAPHS PROVIDED BY
LARRIE S. CURRY, CURATOR OF THE SHAKER VILLAGE
OF PLEASANT HILL

THE ANANDA K. COOMARASWAMY REVIEW
REPRINTED BY PERMISSION OF BERNADETTE COOMARASWAMY

The publisher also acknowledges *Figures of Speech or Figures of Thought?
The Traditional View of Art* by Ananda K. Coomeraswamy,
published by World Wisdom, 2007, where the
Ananda K. Coomaraswamy review also appears.

Excerpts from *The Hidden Ground of Love: The Letters of Thomas Merton
on Religious Experience and Social Concerns* by Thomas Merton,
edited by William H. Shannon, Copyright © 1985
by the Merton Legacy Trust, reprinted by permission
of Farrar, Straus and Giroux, LLC.

BROADSTONE BOOKS
AN IMPRINT OF BROADSTONE MEDIA LLC
418 ANN STREET
FRANKFORT, KY 40601-1929
BroadstoneBooks.com

For Robert and Brendan

for all the many Angels in my life

CONTENTS

INTRODUCTION

Thomas Merton was once advised by Evelyn Waugh, who edited the British edition of *The Seven Storey Mountain* published as *Elected Silence,* to "put books aside and write serious letters and to make an art of it."* The seriousness of Merton's letter writing and the art he made of it can now be grasped to some extent with the publication over recent years of a variety of collections of his letters.

In his own lifetime Merton had been the first editor of his own letters with his mimeographed collection of the *Cold War Letters,* his exchange of letters on monastic issues with Ronald Roloff, OSB, and in preparing a selection of his letters to his Columbia classmate and friend Bob Lax for publication.‡ In his Legacy Trust, Merton also made provision for further collections of his letters to be published. The five volumes of Merton's correspondence published under the general editorship of William H. Shannon contains over 2,200 letters written by Thomas Merton to a wide variety of correspondents. Further volumes of letters have been published containing both sides of the correspondence between Merton and figures such as James Laughlin, Robert Lax,

---

*Thomas Merton, *The Hidden Ground of Love: The Letters of Thomas Merton on Religious Experience and Social Concerns,* selected and edited by William H. Shannon (New York: Farrar, Straus and Giroux, 1985), vi.

‡Thomas Merton and Robert Lax, *A Catch of Anti-Letters* (Mission, Kansas: Sheed, Andrews and McMeel, 1978).

Jean Leclercq, Czeslaw Milosz, Boris Pasternak, Rosemary Ruether, Jonathan Greene, and D. T. Suzuki.

For the last five years of his life Merton kept the majority of the letters he received and carbon copies of most of the letters he wrote and these are now preserved at the Thomas Merton Center at Bellarmine University in Louisville, Kentucky. In the years prior to this, publication of the letters Merton wrote has been dependent on his correspondents making the letters he wrote to them known and available for publication. Over the years many unpublished letters have come to light from a great variety of sources. The Thomas Merton Center now holds correspondence to over 2,100 individual correspondents ranging from single letters to exchanges of over five hundred pieces of correspondence.

Between the years 1960 and 1964 Thomas Merton corresponded with Edward Deming Andrews and then, after Andrews' death in 1964, for a short time he corresponded with his widow, Faith Andrews.

Merton's correspondence with Edward Deming Andrews, the renowned Shaker scholar, was initiated by Andrews in late November 1960. Andrews later recalled he had read *The Seven Storey Mountain* and had heard Mark Van Doren, a mutual friend, speak frequently of Thomas Merton. But they "longed to know him" and when Andrews heard of Merton's interest in writing a book on the Shakers to be illustrated by photographs taken by Shirley Burden he "finally wrote him, offering assistance on the book project."* Merton had worked with Burden on the book *God is My Life: The Story of Our Lady of Gethsemani* which was published in 1960, and although the project to work on a book about

---

*Edward Deming Andrews and Faith Andrews, *Fruits of the Shaker Tree of Life: Memoirs of Fifty Years of Collecting and Research* (Stockbridge, MA: Berkshire Traveller Press, 1975), 170.

the Shakers together was discussed in Merton's correspondence with Burden, nothing ever came of it. Many of Merton's own photographs of Pleasant Hill have been preserved, however, and a selection of these are reproduced in this volume.

In responding to the letter from Edward Deming Andrews Merton mentions he had also been waiting for an opportunity to write to him and that he already knew a number of Andrews' books including *The People Called Shakers* and *Shaker Furniture*. Merton's generous reply to Andrews initiated an all too brief, but substantial, exchange of correspondence which was cut short by the death of Edward Deming Andrews on June 13, 1964.

In January 1964 Edward Deming Andrews wrote to Merton in response to an article on the Shakers Merton had written which was published in the journal *Jubilee*. In the same letter Andrews asked Merton to write a brief introduction to a new book he was writing on Shaker furniture. In requesting Merton to write this introduction Andrews said of Merton "I know of no one who has caught so truthfully the spirit which animated the Shaker crafts-men." Merton accepted Andrews' invitation although he notes he had been refusing such invitations lately, however, he says, "I love the Shakers and all that they have left us far too much to be able to say no." Edward Deming Andrews sent Merton a copy of the manuscript of *Religion in Wood* on March 24th, 1964 so that Merton could read the text prior to writing his introduction.

Merton did not get around to writing his introduction to *Religion in Wood* until July 1964 by which time Edward Deming Andrews had died. After the rumor of Edward Deming Andrews' death was confirmed for Merton in the monastery, he wrote to Faith Andrews in late July offering words of consolation to her and praise for her husband's work. Merton's friend, also his former professor from his days at Columbia University, Mark Van Doren, likewise spoke highly of the work of Edward Deming Andrews saying that he restored dignity to the word "authority" and "he knew more about the Shakers than anyone ever has... he knew about them; he knew of them; he knew them" writing that "he loved them: not sentimentally, not nostalgically, but with an abiding respect for the ideas their entire life expressed." Words which undoubtedly account for Merton's friendship with the Andrews and the rapport that can be seen in their correspondence.

In his letter of condolence to Faith Andrews Merton also assured her that after some delays the preface to *Religion in Wood* was finished and was being retyped. In this preface, described by Merton as "an essay in its own right," he made the perceptive, enigmatic and frequently quoted statement that "the peculiar grace of a Shaker chair is due to the fact that it was made by someone capable of believing than an angel might come and sit on it."

After receiving the preface Faith wrote to Merton saying how beautiful she found it, adding she had read it every day since it arrived, "almost a month ago." Merton corresponded with Faith Andrews a few times in the subsequent months with the last extant piece of correspondence dating from April 1965 in which Merton asked about progress in her plans to publish *Religion in Wood*. *Religion in Wood* was eventually published in 1966 by Indiana University Press.

The letters in this short volume are a wonderful exchange and give the reader a fine example of Merton's empathy and deep harmony with his correspondent that are witnessed to in so many of his letters and in the accounts by those who knew Merton of their friendships with him. A sense of this was recorded by Andrews in his account of his November 1961 visit to the Abbey of Gethsemani when Merton met Edward Deming Andrews and Faith Andrews for the first and only time. They were in Kentucky at the invitation of Ralph McCallister who was at that time executive director of the organization working to restore Pleasant Hill.

They visited Merton at Gethsemani, and Merton had the opportunity to discuss the plans for the restoration of Pleasant Hill. In a memoir published posthumously Andrews recalled his visit to Gethsemani writing:

> The visit to the Trappist monastery was a memorable one. At Father Merton's suggestion we arrived in time to attend the short choral office of Nones which was chanted at 1:15 in the afternoon. We met the good brother in a room reserved for visitors, and then he took me on a tour of the Abbey. (The rules forbade Faith from accompanying us.) Though the monastic rule of silence prevailed, in his role as guide and director of novices he was permitted to speak, answering all questions most graciously and with deep insight into the dedicated work of the order. In the book store we selected a volume we wanted to buy – *God is My Life,* with photographs of Gethsemani by Shirley Burden and a forward by Thomas Merton – but he insisted on presenting it to us. "You can buy books elsewhere," he said, "but not here." Nor would he take money for the famed Trappist cheese, so Faith put the money in the poor box. After an hour or so of the best of good talk, we took our leave, gently waved away by one whom we had already come to regard as a spiritual mentor and intimate friend.[*]

In recent years Edward Deming and Faith Andrews have at times been criticized for having taken advantage of the Shakers from whom they bought much of the Shaker furniture they owned and for a lack of appropriate scholarship. However, their work was essential in preserving, and making known, the Shaker legacy.

---

[*]Andrews, *Fruits of the Shaker Tree of Life,* 172.

Without their devotion and work much might have been lost. From the letters in this collection it is possible to see clearly the heart of their interest and their deep love for the Shakers.

It is evident from these letters the enthusiasm that both writers felt for the Shakers and the high regard in which they both held each other. As Andrews writes to Merton in November 1963: "you have constantly been in my thoughts – always near, and always a true friend and guide" words reminiscent of those Andrews wrote after his visit to Gethsemani describing how they were "gently waved away by one whom we had already come to regard as a spiritual mentor and intimate friend." In a similar fashion Merton spoke highly of Andrews writing to Faith Andrews after the death of Edward Deming Andrews that "Ted was faithful to his call, and his work has born more fruit than we can estimate on this earth. His reward will surely be with those angelic ones whose work and life he understood and shared."

After Thomas Merton's first visit to Pleasant Hill in June 1959 he recorded in his personal journal that "there is a lot of Shakertown in Gethsemani." This undoubtedly served as another reason for the affinity between Merton and Andrews. Merton recognized in the Shakers, and in the Shaker buildings and furniture at Pleasant Hill, something of the Cistercian spirit he worked to cultivate, or more accurately, recultivate at the Abbey of Gethsemani and in the larger Cistercian world. Similarly in Merton, and in the monastic life at Gethsemani, Andrews found something of the Shaker spirit of which he had for so long been a scholar, preserver and aficionado.

In this volume of correspondence we are invited to partake with Thomas Merton and Edward Deming and Faith Andrews both in their enthusiasm and their affection, for the Shakers and for each other, and to join with them in the Communion of Saints and in the Shaker belief in the spiritual presence of their departed believers. Their correspondence manifests a rare meeting of spirits, indeed it is the celebration of a meeting of angels.

A MEETING OF ANGELS

THE LETTERS OF

THOMAS MERTON AND

EDWARD DEMING ANDREWS

EDWARD DEMING ANDREWS
TO THOMAS MERTON

November 29, 1960

Dear Brother Thomas,

Word has reached me that you are writing a book on the religion of the Shakers, to be illustrated by Shirley Burden.* I am deeply interested in this culture, as you may know, and would be happy to be of any assistance. Please feel free to call upon me.

Our attention was called to the Trappists of Gethsemane [*sic*] several months ago. Through Mr. Harold Hugo of the Meriden (Conn.) Gravure Company, we heard that they were contemplating a project of reproducing Shaker furniture. This may have been hearsay, but if not, we would like to know more about it.

The enclosed may be of interest to you.‡

With very best wishes,

Sincerely yours.

---

*Merton had worked with Shirley C. Burden on *God Is My Life: The Story of Our Lady of Gethsemani* which was published in 1960. Although the project to work on a book about the Shakers was discussed in Merton's correspondence with Burden, nothing ever came of it.

‡Andrews sent Merton a catalog of an exhibit of his Shaker Inspirational Drawings that was currently touring the North-Eastern United States.

THOMAS MERTON TO
EDWARD DEMING ANDREWS

December 12, 1960

Dear Mr. Andrews:

It was indeed a pleasure to get your kind letter. I had been thinking of writing to you myself for some time, as I know several of your fine books on the Shakers and indeed have the two most important ones here. (I take it that *The People Called Shakers* and *Shaker Furniture* are among your most important studies.) So first of all I want to express my gratitude to you for the fine work you have done and are doing. I shall certainly have to depend very much on you, if I do any work at all in this field, and I am grateful for your offer of assistance.

It is quite true that Shirley Burden and I have discussed the possibility of a book on the Shakers. My part would not be precisely a study of their religion, if by that is to be understood their doctrines, but of their spirit and I might say their mysticism, in practice, as evidenced by their life and their craftsmanship. To me the Shakers are of very great significance, besides being something of a mystery, by their wonderful integration of the spiritual and the physical in their work. There is no question in my mind that one of the finest and most genuine religious expressions of the nineteenth century is in the silent eloquence of Shaker craftsmanship. I am deeply interested in the thought that a hundred years ago our two communities were so close together, so similar, somehow, in ideals, and yet evidently had no contact with one another. I have seen the buildings of the Shaker colony near Harrodsburg here, and of course it speaks volumes to me. There is at present a plan on foot in which you will be interested: some friends of mine in University circles in Lexington are trying to buy the buildings and preserve them in some form or other, perhaps as a study center. If you are interested I can have them get in touch with you, they are having rather a hard time and you might be able to help them. In fact it might be wise eventually to coordinate the various efforts to save the different Shaker communities everywhere. I wrote a little letter to the Shakers at Canterbury N.H. and got a sweet letter back from one of the old ladies, but I have not pursued the correspondence. I ought to try to write to them for Christmas, though.

But in any case, your letter inspires me to pursue further my studies of the Shakers. I will not rush at it and I will try to profit by their example and put into practice some of their careful and honest principles. It would be a crime to treat them superficially, and without the deepest love, reverence and understanding. There can be so much meaning to a study of this kind: meaning for twentieth century America which has lost so much in the last hundred years—lost while seeming to gain. I think the extinction of the Shakers and of their particular kind of spirit is an awful portent. I feel all the more akin to them because our own Order, the Cistercians, originally had the same kind of ideal of honesty, simplicity, good work, for a spiritual motive.

Now I do want to take advantage of your kind offer. I am still far from getting down to the study I want to do. But if you have any interesting books that are not too precious to lend, which speak of the Shaker spirit in work and living, I would be very happy to borrow them and take care of them. But more urgent than that: I wonder if you could let me have any reproductions of your Shaker inspirational paintings? I would like to use two or three if possible in a book on religious art which is ready for publication.* I think certainly some of the trees of life etc would be most suitable (These I have seen in reproduction) but I do not know about the others. Perhaps there is among them something with a special spiritual quality. I would be glad to use anything you can let me have. Of course you will let me know in what terms the acknowledgement should be printed in the book etc. I am very interested in your project to save the Hancock community and shall pray for its success. In fact I pray God to bless all your work and efforts in this regard.

With very cordial good wishes,

Sincerely yours in Christ.

---

*Merton's book on religious art, provisionally entitled "Art and Worship," was never published.

EDWARD DEMING ANDREWS
TO THOMAS MERTON

December 19, 1960

Dear Brother Thomas Merton:

We so appreciate your letter, with its great understanding and insight. The mystical phases of the Shaker experience need to be explored, and I know of no one who could penetrate the mystery better than you. Rufus Jones might have done so. The Society for Psychic Research, under Walter F. Prince, was once interested. The present-day Shakers themselves, in writing about the origin of their "vision" songs, "gifts," revelations and rituals, leave the question virtually unanswered—as they do the concept of Wisdom, or Holy Mother Wisdom, who is introduced almost casually in their doctrinal expositions. Incidentally, my book, *The Gift to be Simple. Songs, Dances and Rituals of the American Shakers* (J.J. Augustin, New York, 1940) would be a useful source for research in this field. It is now out of print.

I should very much like to honor your request for books and reproductions of the inspirationals. As to the latter, our collection of fourteen drawings and watercolors is now at Smith College, where they will remain until Jan. 25, 1961. If you can make any arrangement with Mr. Burden, or some one else, to have a color reproduction or silk screen done of one or two of them while they are there, you have our permission—and we would of course leave the acknowledgment to you. I have a manuscript on the subject— "Visions of the Heavenly Sphere"—which I hope will be published if sponsorship can be arranged. Nothing definite yet. The only articles are one I did for *The Antiques Magazine* (December, 1945), illustrated in black and white, and one in *Portfolio Magazine,* Zebra Press, 22 East 12th St., Cincinnati, (Vol. II, No. 1, Winter, 1950) in which there are four plates in color. A few years ago Allen Saalburg (Canal Press, Frenchtown, N.J.) did three silk screens (Tree of Life, A Bower of Mulberry Trees, and An Emblem of the Heavenly Sphere), which are still listed in his catalogue, though we were given to understand that the first one is no longer available, and the last does not include all of the emblems in the original document.

As for books that "speak of the Shaker spirit in work and living," I can think of none exclusively devoted to this theme, though there are many such passages in the extensive literature on the order. *A Summary View of the Millennial Church,* by Elders Seth Y. Wells and Calvin Green (Albany, 1823) is a reliable account of "the general principles of their faith and testimony." I would be happy to loan you a copy.

The project for preserving the lovely colony at Pleasant Hill is a worthy one which I would be glad to forward in any way I can. Did you know that for some time Mr. Barry Bingham, editor of the Louisville *Courier-Journal* (and his father before him) have been interested in protecting this property? I understand that the Blue Grass Trust for Historic Preservation is currently making efforts to get options on the land and buildings. Our collection was once slated to go there.

A colleague of mine recently wrote an article in *Perspecta* (published here at Yale) on the architecture of the Cistercians, and I know what you mean when you speak of the honesty and simplicity of their work, and how akin that was to the Shakers'. I copied three of their orders, or laws, which could have been written by the Believers themselves:

"Everything above an absolute minimum is superfluous and has to be discarded."

"We want none of the superfluities which would deform the honesty of an old religious order."

"Being a 'workshop for the art of holiness,' it should be a structure without '*affectus*.'"

It is strange that there was no contact between your order and the Shakers. As you know, there is a Benedictine priory at South Union, Ky. occupying the Shaker buildings there. They have a deep respect for the Shaker traditions and are forming a library of materials relating to that Shaker colony.

I am enclosing two little pamphlets which may be of interest to you. We would like you to have them.

One thing more. In your letter you have expressed so finely the importance of preserving the spirit of Shaker craftsmanship that I wonder if you would mind, if occasion arises, if we quoted briefly from it in our literature on the Hancock project. If this is not possible, I will understand.

Please feel free to ask me any questions and call on me for any assistance. It will be a privilege to help.

Sincerely yours.

enc.
Shaker Order of Christmas
Shaker Herbs and Herbalists

PS One other possibility on the inspirationals. Three of ours were photographed in color for a Carnegie Study of the visual arts—primarily for slides. They are being processed and developed by SANDA K, 39 West 53rd St., New York 19. We haven't received the one of the drawings yet, but they might be ready.

THOMAS MERTON TO
EDWARD DEMING ANDREWS

January 17, 1961

Dear Mr. Andrews:

This morning I received a good long letter from Shirley Burden in California and some pictures he took of the Shaker buildings and graveyard at Harvard. I was very glad to hear from him after a long silence, and to know that he was still interested in our project. He told me also of the proposed exhibition that is being planned by the Museum of Modern Art for 1962 which will include photographs and probably furniture etc. I am sure you know all about this.

Today therefore seems to be a good time to answer your kind letter of December 19th and to thank you for the two charming little booklets. The one on herbs and herbalists is particularly charming, and again it brings to mind the similarity of ideals and practices which bring Shakers and Cistercians closer together. Unfortunately we do not grow our own medicinal herbs today at least in America, but St. Bernard wanted the monks of Tre Fontane near Rome to do so. Or rather, to be more exact, he wanted them *not* to "seek out doctors and swallow their nostrums" but to "use common herbs such as are used by the poor". (Letter 388, in the B.S. James translation, 1953) The study of the use of herbs by the medieval Cistercians would be quite interesting, I am sure.

One of Shirley Burden's photos is of a stone barn near Harvard which is very Cistercian indeed—an old Shaker barn. There are many interesting statutes of the General Chapters concerning architecture, decoration etc. I am having the brothers at the gatehouse send you a booklet called *The Spirit of Simplicity* which has interesting material and lots of references. I think you would like to have it to refer to. Please forgive the fact that it is not very well designed or printed. I think I will also send you my booklet *Monastic Peace* about the purposes and ideals of the Order.

Certainly a Cistercian ought to be in a good position to understand the Shaker spirit, and I do hope that with leisure, study and meditation I will eventually be able to do something on this wonderful subject. I would like to borrow the volume you suggest, Elders Wells and Green's *Summary View of the Millennial Church*. The trouble is that I lack so much of the background of what one might, for want of a better term, describe as the "gnostic" element that came down through unrecorded, oral traditions and eventually reached people like Mother Ann. I did my thesis on Blake when I was in the graduate school at Columbia, and this would count as a start, but it was long ago.

At the moment I am working on a subject that runs parallel to the Shaker interest that I have and it may in the long run help a great deal. I am in touch with Mrs Ananda Coomaraswamy and am looking into the remarkable collection of material that he left, not only on Oriental art but on philosophy and spirituality. In order to keep from spreading myself over too wide an area, I am trying to concentrate on this field for the moment.

Before I go any further I want to say that you have my full permission to quote from my letter about the importance of preserving Shaker craftsmanship. If anything I have said can be of the slightest help, I will be delighted. Also I do not think I answered a question you asked in your first letter: as to whether the monks here were reproducing Shaker pieces of furniture. No, indeed we are not. We are very busy with a big job of renovation in our old buildings and our carpenters are all engaged in this. We have one very good cabinet maker but his work is nothing like Shaker furniture. I know that one of our Brother carpenters is very interested in Shaker work, however.

The closest we are getting is that a friend of mine, a layman, is copying an old Shaker school desk from a reproduction in the book on New England Pine Furniture, for me.* This I hope to use in a hermitage in the woods. It is just possible that some rumor about this got around, and led to your surmise that the monks were now reproducing Shaker pieces. But we are not.

I know of the Benedictine Priory at South Union and hope to have more contact with them. As to the contacts between our Fathers here and the former colony at Pleasant Hill, there is quite a distance between us and in those days I hardly think any of the monks would have had much occasion to go over that way. I should say it was about sixty miles over hilly country. I can imagine one of our Breton founders perhaps having to go to Lexington through Pleasant Hill, and being somewhat perplexed as he drove through in his wagon. The language barrier would in itself have created an obstacle if nothing else. It was a long time before our first monks became naturalized so to speak, and Americans did not join the community until the end of the 19th century.

I have not been in touch with Barry Bingham, but I might discuss the Pleasant Hill project with him later on. The people who are interested in the idea, in Lexington, tell me that the owners have banded together and put up such a big price that there is no hope for the moment of anything being done. Perhaps one or

---

*Merton is here referring to a writing table designed for him by the painter and typographer Victor Hammer and built by David Rowland.

another of these friends of the Pleasant Hill colony may get in touch with you. I hope it will eventually be saved. There is a wonderful character of solitude and loneliness about the hilltop site looking out over rolling country. I was deeply moved looking out of the attic of the old Guest House through the branches of a big cedar at the quiet field in which they used to dance (Holy Sion's plain). Incidentally in an offprint of Coomaraswamy I ran across a lovely old carol, about the "dancing" of God with man in the mystery of the Incarnation. I think here there may be an important lead. The carol is an ancient English one. In it, the Lord speaks of His coming at Christmas in the following words: "Tomorrow is my dancing day…" I do not have the text at my elbow, one of the other Fathers has borrowed it.

Your study on the "Visions of the Heavenly Sphere" sounds very absorbing and I hope I shall one day see it in print.* Do you by any chance have offprints of your articles to which you refer, especially in *Portfolio Magazine?* I suppose these magazines do not give offprints, but I believe I can find them in the Louisville Library. I am much handicapped in a study of this kind by the fact that we travel very very little indeed and never very far afield. Hence I have to rely on the kindness of those who are willing to lend me things.

I have seen your book *The Gift to be Simple* referred to in many places, and that too I want to read some day. I shall not borrow it now, since I may be able to get it in town. And in any case it must wait a bit.

In working on the Shakers I would certainly not make any sense if I let myself be hurried and crowded and confused by multiplicity.

---

*Edward Deming Andrews and Faith Andrews, V*isions of the Heavenly Sphere, A Study in Shaker Religious Art* (Charlottesville, VA: Published for the Henry Francis du Pont Winterthur Museum by The University Press of Virginia, 1969)

But I hope to continue my reading and study in the things I have on hand and to keep up with the Shakers at the same time. Eventually, at the right time, the two lines will converge and something will result. Meanwhile I am very happy to be in touch with you, and I want to keep in touch. An exchange of ideas will be most profitable, and it is possible that something might materialize—for instance some project to which I might make a small contribution. Please consider me a willing and interested collaborator in anything that will help preserve the spirit and skill of Shaker craftsmanship and ways of life.

With cordial good wishes for the New Year.

Sincerely yours in Christ.

EDWARD DEMING ANDREWS
TO THOMAS MERTON

February 13, 1961

Dear Brother Thomas Merton—or should I write you as Father Louis?

I am deeply grateful for the pamphlets and the little book you so kindly sent me. In reading them I am constantly made aware how closely allied, in many respects, are the ideals of the Shakers and the monastic orders. I would like to know who did the line drawings in your *Monastic Peace.* They are so very lovely, so fraught with meaning! I came across a reference to Brother Antonius in yesterday's *Times,* in a review by Kenneth Rexroth.

It's interesting that you should have Ananda Coomaraswamy's papers. He wrote what we thought was the most understanding and scholarly review of our book on Shaker Furniture. (*The Art Bulletin,* Vol. XXI, 1939) A year or so before it came out he visited us at our farm in Richmond, Mass. and attended one of our early exhibits at the Berkshire Museum in Pittsfield. I have always liked what he had to say about the arts, as in his article on "The Nature of Medieval Art": that there used to be no distinction between fine and applied art, or pure and decorative art. "All art was for 'good use' (a Shaker term) and 'adapted to condition.' But could be applied either to noble or common uses, but was no more or less art in the one case than in the other... Perfection, rather than beauty, was the end in view." That was Shaker philosophy too.

Another person who was sensitive to the spirit of Shaker craftsmanship was our, and your friend, Mark Van Doren.* His review of our book, in *The Nation,* was entitled "Religion in Wood."

I would like sometime to have a copy of the old English carol in which the Lord speaks of His "dancing day"—or at least the reference.

I am sending you a copy of *A Summary View of the Millennial Church,* which you may return at your convenience. Also one of the catalogues that Smith College put out at the time of our exhibit. I haven't seen a report of the symposium. However, the Shaker Festival, or Meeting, in which the glee club and drama departments of Smith and Amherst participated, was taped. This tape is available (for $3.50 I think) by writing to Mr. Vincent Braun of the theater department at Smith. It was an inspiring experience.

In reference to what St. Bernard said about doctors, it is interesting to note what the Shaker Millennial Laws had to say on the same subject: "The order of God forbids that Believers should employ doctors of the world, except in some extreme cases, or the case of a sick child, whose parents are among the world, and desire such aid." According to *The Testimonies...* (1816) "Brethren and Sisters who visited the Church under tribulation and sufferings, whether of body or mind, were often instantly released, by a mere touch of the hand from Mother, even by the touch of her finger, or the sound of her voice." The use of medicinal herbs was of course common in their own "nurse shops."

With warmest regards,

Sincerely.

---

*Mark Van Doren taught Merton English at Columbia University. They corresponded until Merton's death in 1968 and Van Doren was instrumental in the publication of Merton's first book, *Thirty Poems.*

THOMAS MERTON TO
EDWARD DEMING ANDREWS

August 22, 1961

Dear Mr. Andrews:

It is a terribly long time since you last wrote and since you sent the little book on the *Millennial Church*. I should have answered you long ago. And I should also have returned the book by this time. I am at last answering and it is in order to accuse myself of slothfulness and lethargy, and ask your indulgence so that I may keep the book a little while longer.

To excuse myself, I can point to the condition of our times, which no one, not even a monk, completely escapes or transcends. I have allowed myself to be involved in more tasks and interests than I should, and the one that has most suffered has been the study of the Shakers. It is in a way so completely out of the theological realm with which I am familiar, although their spirit has so much in common with ours. This makes me hesitant to plunge in deeply, and so I turn to other things in which I feel I can accomplish something. Thus I can tell myself that I have not "wasted time." Yet slow and patient work that does not immediately produce a result is no waste of time… I am hoping that I can get back to this kind of study of the Shaker sources later in the fall.

Yet perhaps some of my other interests may remotely cast a light on this study. I am currently very interested in Clement of

Alexandria, one of the earliest Christian "gnostics," and his spirit has much in common with that of Shaker simplicity and joy. Then too I am acquainting myself with the magnificent work on primitive religions that has been done by Mircea Eliade. In reality I think he is the one most qualified to give a complete, well rounded appreciation of the Shaker doctrines, practices and spirit. Perhaps some day he will come down here and I will be able to get him interested. It is very certain that the Shakers preserved many many deeply important religious symbols and lived out some of the most basic religious myths in their Christian and gnostic setting. I cannot help feeling also that the very existence of the Shakers at that particular moment of history has a very special significance, a sort of "prophetic" function in relation to what has come since.

How are the last Shakers up in New Hampshire? I often think of them. I have intended to write to the Eldress but I have so little time to write letters that have to be written that none is left for those that would be mere luxury.

I was happy to see your allusions to Mark Van Doren and to Coomaraswamy in your last letter (as understanding reviewers of your fine book on *Shaker Furniture*). Mark is coming down to Louisville in the fall and I hope he will be out here. Coomaraswamy has—as far as my study of him is concerned—remained on the shelf. I have not given up but...

The carol "Tomorrow will be my dancing day" is to be found in any good collection of English carols, I believe. My reference was to a little introduction by A. Coomaraswamy to a translation of the Hindu religious play the "Taking of Toll," printed in London in 1915. If you cannot trace this carol I will be happy to send you a copy of what I have of it, which is incomplete.

Everything regarding Shakers is always of great interest to me. I think often of them, of the extinct colony that was so near here: I think of their simplicity and their mystical fervor. It is always to me a deeply significant thought, and I feel deeply related to them in some kind of obscure communion. I understand that some manuscripts relating to this colony are in the Filson Club in Louisville. I intend to go and look at them. Meanwhile this may attract you to this part of the world. I hope it does.

The copy of the Shaker schoolboy desk which is in our hermitage is a pure joy.

With every best wish, and with the expression of my gratitude and friendship in the Spirit,

Cordially yours.

PS I know you will forgive the clumsiness of my typing. I type like a newspaperman with four fingers and quite fast. You see the result.

EDWARD DEMING ANDREWS
TO THOMAS MERTON

August 26, 1961

Dear Brother Thomas Merton:

It was good to hear from you again. Aside from our common interest in the Shaker culture, I feel close to you as a person, and treasure the spirit which breathes through your letters.

As to the book, *The Millennial Church,* we would like you to keep it, to study it at your convenience, and eventually, if you wish, to add it to the Abbey's library. If other basic Shaker works are needed for research, by you or others, we would be happy to be of service. Among the Shakers in Ohio and Kentucky were three biblical scholars—Richard McNemar, John Dunlavy and Bishop Harvey Eades—whose works I feel are important to an understanding of Shaker thought. I would very much like to read Mircea Eliade's work on primitive religions. It should be at the Yale library.

As you will see by the enclosures,* our own work has shifted from New Haven to the Berkshires. The Hancock colony is a beautiful place, and its restoration, though not without its problems (financial and otherwise), is a challenge with great rewards. Our purpose is to try to restore not only the buildings but something of the spirit which once pervaded this peaceful settlement.

Another project in restoration, as you may know, is well under

---

*Andrews enclosed for Merton a pamphlet describing the plans to save the Shaker Village of Hancock in Massachusetts.

way at Pleasant Hill, Kentucky. There is great interest there, at the University of Kentucky and other places, and the Blue Grass Trust has now obtained an option on the property. Barry Bingham, publisher of the Louisville *Courier-Journal*, recently sent us an article, with color illustrations, which confirms our opinion that it is one of the most attractive Shaker societies. If and when the project materializes, Kentucky—with its little museum at Auburn and the buildings at South Union already preserved by the Benedictines—will increasingly attract people interested in this unique aspect of American history. We hope to make a pilgrimage to Pleasant Hill this fall after the opening of two Shaker rooms at Winterthur.

With warmest regards.

encl.   6 tracts
            flyer
            Hancock History

EDWARD DEMING ANDREWS
TO THOMAS MERTON

November 10, 1961

Dear Thomas Merton:

You were so good to give of your time and thought to us at the Abbey.* I wish it were possible to tell you how profoundly moved we were by the experience. Suffice it to say that it was a rare privilege to have met with you, and to visit a place so imbued with the spirit of Christian love.

On the plane back to Rochester I read—more than once—the typescript on Clement of Alexandria. Now I have read, and pondered, your other gift, *God is My Life*—and want, all the more, to have Mr. Burden, or some one else equally sensitive to the spirit of place, to do something like this on the Shaker theme—before the culture is extinct. We have a good collection of early stereographs, many of which are fine prints, but these should be supplemented by pictures which capture mood and landscape and the often elusive spirit of a community.

Under separate cover I am sending you a copy of our book on Shaker furniture.‡

---

*On November 6th 1961 Edward Deming Andrews and his wife Faith, accompanied by Ralph McCallister, the executive director of the organization working to restore Pleasant Hill, visited Thomas Merton at the Abbey of Gethsemani.

With warmest best wishes, and again our deep appreciation of your kindness to us.

Sincerely.

---

‡Edward Deming Andrews and Faith Andrews, *Shaker Furniture, The Craftsmanship of an American Communal Sect* (New York: Dover Publications, 1950). Andrews inscribed the volume: "For Thomas Merton and his Trappist brethren—in appreciation of a memorable day at the Abbey of Gethsemani in November, 1961. With love, Edward and Faith Andrews."

THOMAS MERTON TO
EDWARD DEMING ANDREWS

December 21, 1961

Dear Edward:

Forgive please this very long delay in thanking you for the copy of *Shaker Furniture* which will remain a highly valued possession in the novitiate library.

I believe it is of the highest importance for the novices to see these things, and get used to this wonderful simplicity. This wordless simplicity, in which the works of quiet and holy people speak humbly for themselves. How important that is in our day when we are flooded with a tidal wave of meaningless words: and worse still when in the void of those words the sinister power of hatred and destruction is at work. The Shakers remain as witnesses to the fact that only humility keeps man in communion with truth, and first of all with his own inner truth. This one must know without knowing it, as they did. For as soon as a man becomes aware of "his truth" he lets go of it and embraces an illusion.

I am so glad you liked Clement. If it ever gets printed, I will gladly send you a copy.* New Directions is not in a hurry to decide because we are working on a more urgent project, a book of articles against nuclear war.

Clement of Alexandria: Selections from the Protreptikos, an essay and translation by Thomas Merton was published by New Directions in 1962.

Speaking of Clement and Alexandria, you know of Philo Judaeus, the Jewish Platonist who flourished in that city. He has a very intriguing book *De Therapeutis* (which I have not yet found and read). In this book he speaks of Jewish monastic communities in Egypt in which there are some similarities with the Shakers. Particularly the fact that they were contemplative communities of men and women, living separately and joining in worship, though separated by a partition. It would seem there might be many interesting facts in this book, and I recommend it to your curiosity. Alexandria remains a fascinating place, and I am sure that more study of the intellectual and spiritual movements that flourished there will prove very rewarding.

Perhaps I can hope to hear from Shirley Burden at Christmas. I would have written to him long ago but he has moved and I do not have his new address. I badly want him to get here in the spring and take those pictures. Do you by any chance have his address? I think he has been in touch with you, but some time ago.

Are there any further possibilities of getting the Shaker spirituals down here? Should I contact the curator of the Speed museum in Louisville?

Without trying to rush this to you by Christmas, I am just sending it along with two tokens of friendship, a short article on peace and an excerpt on the "cosmic dance"* from the Christmas *Jubilee*. They will not reach you until New Year, perhaps. But in any case my prayers and good wishes to you and Mrs. Andrews come with them. It was a very great pleasure to have you here with us for an afternoon and I hope you will be back again one of these days.

Very cordially in Christ Our Lord.

---

*"The General Dance," *Jubilee*, 9 (December 1961): 8-11, subsequently included in *New Seeds of Contemplation*.

EDWARD DEMING ANDREWS
TO THOMAS MERTON

August 6, 1962

Dear Brother Thomas,

Please do not think because I have not written that I have not had you often in mind. In a talk I gave this spring to a group of guides and guests at Winterthur, on the subject of Shaker Culture —The Forces Behind the Forms, I took the liberty of quoting from one of your letters. The theme of interior and exterior simplicity is one with great germinal significance, and I come back again and again, in my work, to ideas from Gethsemane. [*sic*] You have a secure place in our hearts.

My immediate purpose in writing is to tell you that I am sending, under separate cover, a copy of the paperback issue of *The Gift to be Simple,** also a little pamphlet on the meeting house which we moved to Hancock this spring. It still needs to be restored and will probably not be dedicated until late fall or next spring, at which time I hope that I can again have a message from you—if not you in person. There is a beautiful early Shaker hymn called "The Living Building," the text for which was first published in Hancock, which I would like to have sung at the dedication, after the traditional covenant is read.

---

*Edward Deming Andrews, *The Gift to Be Simple: Songs, Dances and Rituals of the American Shakers* (New York: Dover Publications, 1962).

Have you had an opportunity to do your projected photo essay on Shawnee Run (Pleasant Hill or Shakertown)? We haven't heard much about the restoration there, but assume that it is going forward.

With warmest regards.

THOMAS MERTON TO
EDWARD DEMING ANDREWS

September 20, 1962

Dear Edward:

Probably my silence is the result of a more or less frantic effort to preserve some simplicity in my exterior life by only writing letters when I can think about them. Or rather, by trying to convince myself that it is possible to do this when, in reality, it is not possible. So I write business letters under pressure and leave the things I would really like to write until it is too late to write them. Thus I am afflicted with the modern disease, which you perhaps have escaped better than I, although I am supposed to be a monk.

The Gift to be Simple is a book of inestimable value to me. It has in it so many things that move one by their clarity and truth. The "Gift to be simple" is in fact the "Gift to be true," and what we need most in our life today, personal, national and international, is this truth. Some of the songs are naive, all of them are charming by their honesty, but there is one which contains great power: "Decisive Work."* There is more in this than just a pious song.

I shall continue to enjoy these songs and ponder over them. How beautiful is the Meeting House you have moved over to Hancock. I wish I could be there for its dedication: or at least to see it some time. Perhaps I will.

The story of the Shirley Meeting house is filled with conflict and paradox. At this one need not be surprised, because the law of all spiritual life is the law of risk and struggle, and possible failure. There is something significant in the fact that the Shaker ideal was to most people all but impossible, and that therefore it was inevitable that many good men should fall crashing out of the edifice they had helped to build. God alone understands those failures, and knows in what way perhaps they were not failures. Perhaps somewhere in the mystery of Shaker "absolutism" which in many ways appears to be "intolerant" and even arbitrary, there is an underlying gentleness and tolerance and understanding that appears not in words but in life and in work. It is certainly in the songs. Some of us only learn tolerance and understanding after having been intolerant and "absolute." In a word, it is hard to live with a strict and sometimes almost absurd ideal, and the ambivalence involved can be tragic, or salutary. More than anyone else, the Shakers faced that risk and the fruitfulness of their life was a sign of approval upon their daring.

No, I have not settled down to the photo essay. If I did it now, it would be too superficial. I must read and think more. The pictures were taken before any restoration began. I haven't heard much about the progress there, but there does not seem to be a great deal of enthusiasm about it. Let us hope that all will turn out well, worthy of the dear people who left us this monument of truth.

As ever, with the most cordial good wishes to you both in Christ Jesus.

---

*"I have come, / And I've not come in vain. / I have come to sweep / The house of the Lord / Clean, clean, for I've come / And I've not come in vain. / With my broom in my hand, / With my fan and my flail, / This work I will do / And I will not fail, / For lo! I have come / And I've not come in vain." Edward Deming Andrews, *The Gift to be Simple: Songs, Dances and Rituals of the American Shakers* (New York: Dover Publications, 1962), 60.

EDWARD DEMING ANDREWS
TO THOMAS MERTON

December 13, 1962

Dear Brother Thomas,

The song you particularly liked, "Decisive Work," did not have, in my book, the music to which it was sung. I have copied it verbatim from the original MS. and send it to you with our warmest Christmas greetings.

We have read "Grace's House"* to so many of our friends, and given them copies. It is delightful in itself. For us the overtones are full of meaning.

I am working on a piece tentatively entitled *Sheeler and the Shakers* which will include, I hope, about 10 or 15 black and whites which Charles Sheeler did on the Shaker theme.‡

Do you know Armin Landeck, the artist? He is a close friend of Mark Van Doren. This fall he came to Hancock and took about sixty-five photographs which are unusually evocative of the spirit of the village. In its *"Rediscovery"* issue sometime next year *Art in America* plans to use a selection from the portfolio. Armin's sensitive work reminds us of Shirley Burden's. *God is My Life* is one of our great treasures.

---

*Thomas Merton, *Selected Poems of Thomas Merton* (New York: New Directions, 1967), 110-11.
‡Charles Sheeler (1883-1965), American Modernist artist and photographer. The Andrews' essay appeared in *Art in America* 1 (1965): 590-95.

The dedication of the meeting house is scheduled for May 31. I believe our president has already invited two speakers, one an architectural historian and the other a Unitarian minister. If you cannot be here in person, I know you will be in spirit. I would like to read what you wrote about the building in your letter of Sept. 20.

Thank you so much for the calendar, which hangs near my work table and constantly reminds me of the Abbey. And of you.

With best wishes from us both.

THOMAS MERTON TO
EDWARD DEMING ANDREWS

December 28, 1962

Dear Edward:

I was touched at your thoughtfulness in sending me the music for the song "Decisive Work." It is what I would have expected, and I have learned it now, so that I can sing it to myself from time to time when I am alone. I am still deeply convinced that it represents a most important insight into our own time. And of course it is for us in our own way by our faith and obedience to all of God's "words" to attune ourselves to His will and to join in His work, according to our own humble capacities. The Shakers saw this so well, and saw that their work was a cooperation in the same will that framed and governs the cosmos: and more, governs history.

I am so glad you liked "Grace's House." I thought you would. If you would like more copies I can send them.

I do not know Armin Landeck, only of him. I would very much like to see his photographs when they come out. I am now convinced that Shirley Burden has given up any desire, or rather any intention of doing a book on the Shakers. He gets himself in a position where it becomes impossible for him to move and I think that is where he is now, as I get no response to any letters on the subject. I wonder if Armin Landeck would ever think of doing such a book? And if possible, whether I could finally carry out my own intention to write at least a short piece in conjunction with it? I suppose there would still be quite a few obstacles. But it is a thought.

I have not seen Pleasant Hill since the work has been going on, and I have no idea what it is like. There does not seem to be a great deal of enthusiasm over the project in this part of the country.

Your piece on Sheeler does not surprise me. It had not occurred to me that he might have done work on Shaker themes, but of course the connection is obvious. I am sure you will find many interesting things to say and will look forward to reading them.

Did I ever send you a mimeographed book of mine on Peace?* I will put a copy in the mail. It is not, unfortunately, being published.

With cordial wishes to you both for the New Year, in all friendship, in Christ.

----

*Peace in the Post-Christian Era was eventually published by Orbis Books in 2004.

EDWARD DEMING ANDREWS
TO THOMAS MERTON

November 19, 1963

Dear Thomas Merton,

Though I have not written you of late you have constantly been in my thoughts—always near, and always a true friend and guide. Often I turn to your letters, and to your books, especially in these troublous times.

For us they have been troublous too, for we found that we could not condone the policies and behavior of those administering Hancock community, who have power and money but questionable ethics and little real understanding of the Shaker heritage. For two years or so we have tried to maintain our standards, but matters got worse, and finally there was no alternative to our total disassociation with the project. Now we are back to our own independent work again, writing articles, and preparing a supplement to the furniture book and an economic history of the Shakers. Though the culture was in a sense a monk's one, a sub-culture, it is strange how rich it is, and we never seem to exhaust the possibilities of research and interpretation.

We had a wonderful evening not long ago with the Van Dorens, who were visiting the Armin Landecks. We heard Mark again when he read some of Robert Frost's poems at a memorial service at Amherst College.

I am writing this Christmas greeting early as we leave the first week in December for an extended visit with our daughter in California. But warm is the greeting and deep our affection.

Sincerely.

EDWARD DEMING ANDREWS
TO THOMAS MERTON

January 21, 1964

Dear Thomas Merton,

I have been reading with the greatest interest your article on "The Shakers" in *Jubilee*.* Two questions I would like to ask. Is Robert Lax, the roving editor, the Lax of *The Seven Storey Mountain*? And those "sermonettes" on p. 41—"a poor diamond is better than an imitation," etc.—what is their source?

Do you know that the federal government has approved a two million dollar loan for the restoration of Pleasant Hill? This "good news" from Barry Bingham of the Louisville *Courier-Journal*.

I am working to complete a second book on Shaker furniture. I have some eighty or more truly beautiful glossy prints of the furniture, showing 1) pieces by themselves, 2) pieces in Shaker settings, 3) furniture in museum installations, 4) furniture in domestic settings, and 5) a few examples of Ohio-Kentucky craftsmanship. None of this material was illustrated in our first book. The text will consist principally of two essays, "Pure and Simple" and "The Forces Behind the Forms." Dover Publications, Inc. is interested.

Would you consider doing a brief introduction? I know of no

---

*"The Shakers: American Celibates and Craftsmen Who Danced in the Glory of God," *Jubilee* 11 (January 1964): 36-41.

one who has caught so truthfully the spirit which animated the Shaker craftsmen.

With all good wishes—for you and all your brothers in the Abbey.

Sincerely.

THOMAS MERTON TO
EDWARD DEMING ANDREWS

January 29, 1964

Dear Edward:

Thanks for your most recent letter, as well as for the previous one which I put off answering until I thought you might be back from your trip. Thanks also for the book in its new edition, which I am very glad to have. I don't know whether I had written to you saying I was quoting you in the article now in *Jubilee*, but in any case I hope you do not mind my going ahead and using your material. The funny thing is that I took for granted that the "sermonettes" were drawn from something by you. If they are not, then they must be from something in the University of Kentucky Library, on material from Pleasant Hill. I think there are a couple of books I used there which were printed locally about forty years ago, and this probably comes from one of them. I still want to do a little work on the material that is down in this part of the country, such as it is, but do not have time yet. I have a copy now of the ms. of Benjamin Youngs' journey down here, and that should prove interesting.

Now as regards your new book. I would really be delighted to try an introduction. I love the Shakers and all that they have left us far too much to be able to say no, though I have taken to refusing prefaces lately. But in this case I really want to do something. Could I have a look at some of your material when the time comes to write this up?

One thing I have been meaning to consult you about. I am finishing a little book on Art and Worship and would like to include a couple of Shaker prints, at least the Tree of Life. Can you possibly furnish me with pictures of these that will reproduce? I mean one of the Tree of Life and perhaps examples of one or two others (I do not know them well enough to specify which). Also I understand it is now possible to have colored reproductions of the Tree of Life. I would like very much to get one of these to put on the wall. Do you know where I could do this?

Yes, Robert Lax of *Jubilee* is my old friend. At present he is living on a Greek Island, and not roving much or doing much editing, but seems very happy and sends cryptic little poems, a word a line, from his hideout.

I am happy about the federal aid granted to the Pleasant Hill project, that is to say happy in principle. It is good that they have two million dollars, provided that they do the right thing with it. Sometime I will send you some of my photographs of Pleasant Hill (the two in *Jubilee* were mine) you might like to have them on file. I must get prints made. I still cherish slight hopes of doing a little book on Pleasant Hill some day. It will take time. I know that I need the gift to be simple and am inclined enough toward it, so that when I start to get complicated in my projects, I grind to a stop, and have to get the work untangled before it starts up again. I don't think an ambitious Shaker project would fit in with my other commitments at the moment. But some day perhaps.

I am sorry a few simple mistakes crept into the *Jubilee* article, but I will iron them out when it is reprinted in a book, some time in the future.

Best wishes to you both. I am sending a couple of our recent mimeographed items. Sorry my typing is bad, I have a bad arm and am more erratic than usual.

Again, most cordially yours in Christ.

EDWARD DEMING ANDREWS
TO THOMAS MERTON

February 2, 1964

Dear Tom Merton,

We are very happy to know that you will do the preface to our new book. The illustrations—80 to 100 in all—are really lovely, and if they are well reproduced it should be a beautiful volume. The Dover people are interested in publishing it, though their field is chiefly reprints, not original art books. We have a conference with them next week.

When the textual material is in shape I'll send it on. Faith is typing it now.

I have glossy black and white prints of the Tree of Life (1854), Tree of Light or Blazing Tree (1845) and A Bower of Mulberry Trees (1854), which we would be happy to loan to you for use in your book. Let me know and I will send them right on. We will mail you soon, with our love, a silk-screen reproduction of The Tree of Life.

Transparencies or slides in color of three of the inspirationals may be obtained by writing to Sandak, Inc., 39 West 53 Street, New York 19, N.Y. You might wish to direct your request c/o John Waggaman with whom we worked.

Benjamin S. Youngs must have been a remarkable man. As you know, he spent most of his Shaker life as a leader at South Union,

49

Ky. I have his "Journal of One Year" (1805) recording his experience as a missionary opening the gospel in Ohio and Kentucky, also "A Journey to the (Shawnees) Indians..." (1807), which I have transcribed and hope to publish eventually.

With all good wishes,

Sincerely yours.

THOMAS MERTON TO
EDWARD DEMING ANDREWS

March 13, 1964

Dear Ted:

The Tree of Life has arrived, and indeed has been on the wall for some time.* It really brightens up the room and fills the whole place with its own light. I am very happy to have it, and deeply grateful.

Our Lent proceeds quietly but a little hectically as there have been floods near here. The monastery was not affected by them, as it is on high ground, but we had lots of rain, and I always manage to be busier than I would like to be. In the contemplative life one imagines that one would spend all the time absorbed in contemplation, but alas this is not the case. There are always innumerable things to be done and obstacles to getting them done, and large and small troubles.

Did I tell you I got a very interesting set of notes from a Benedictine Nun at Regina Laudis, Bethlehem, Conn. about a visit she and another nun paid to the Shakers at Sabbathday Lake? I am sure you would be very interested. If you do not know Regina Laudis you ought to get to know it. A quite exceptional convent.

---

*Merton's print of The Tree of Life still hangs in his hermitage at the Abbey of Gethsemani.

You should perhaps try to have a conversation with this Sister Prisca, and the Prioress, Mother Benedict, is also a very fine person and would be most interested I think, in speaking to you about the Shakers.

Easter approaches and I keep you and Faith in my thoughts and prayers. May the light and the joy of the Risen Lord shine in your lives through and through.

I thought you might be interested in this message that I wrote to be read to a meeting of Latin American poets in Mexico City.*

Best wishes always, in Christ.

[PS] In a new book I am bringing out I am using sections from letters I had written at one time or another and I want to use a bit out of one of my letters to you about the Shakers. Is that all right? Your name will be mentioned as the recipient of the letter but of course there will be nothing personal in it.‡

---

* "Message to Poets" in *Raids on the Unspeakable* (New York: New Directions, 1966), 155-161.
‡Thomas Merton, *Seeds of Destruction* (New York: Farrar, Straus and Giroux, 1964), 259-261.

EDWARD DEMING ANDREWS
TO THOMAS MERTON

March 19, 1964

Dear Tom,

Your letters do us so much good. The one just received was a true Easter gift!

We're pleased that you like the Tree of Life. Do you still want glossy prints of this one and two others for your projected work on Religion and Art? I have got them out and will send them if you wish.

Faith has nearly completed typing the manuscript of our furniture book. I will send a copy down, as you said you'd like to see the text before writing a preface. It is not long. One chapter is an essay written by the head of the history of art department at the University of Delaware. It is mainly a picture book, with some 80 plates and notes. The title, I think, will be *Religion in Wood. A Second Book of Shaker Furniture.*

Of course it's all right for you to use any excerpt from your letters to me. You will note that in one of my chapters *I* have quoted from *you*. All right?

With all good wishes,
Sincerely.

EDWARD DEMING ANDREWS
TO THOMAS MERTON

Dear Tom,

Enclosed is a copy of the manuscript of "Religion in Wood." I can't tell you how much I appreciate your willingness to write the preface.

We had an inquiry the other day from Doubleday expressing an interest in case we were not committed to another publisher. Another publisher will take it, but I think we'd prefer Doubleday (better reproductions of photographs, perhaps) and plan to see them in a week or so. It was Doubleday who published Shirley Burden's recent book *I Wonder Why*.

Yours with our affection.

Ms. enclosed

THOMAS MERTON TO
EDWARD DEMING ANDREWS

April 5, 1964

Dear Ted:

The ms. has reached me and I want to say it is safe and that I will get to it and to the preface when I have a couple of other urgent jobs out of the way. The title is great and I look forward to getting into it.

About the prints, I will wait until I find out what the publisher wants to do with that art book of mine before I borrow them. The illustrated section is the big problem that is being debated.

Best wishes always,
Cordially yours in Christ.

A MEETING OF ANGELS

—————

THE LETTERS OF
THOMAS MERTON AND
FAITH ANDREWS

THOMAS MERTON TO
FAITH ANDREWS

July 20, 1964

Dear Mrs Andrews:

Some time ago a rumor had reached me that Ted had suddenly been taken from you and from us. I was not able to verify the rumor until recently and I find that it is actually the case. I am shocked and saddened at the news. This is of course a great loss to all of us. He was a bit older than he looked, but I was expecting more work from his pen on the Shakers. Unfortunately that has been cut short.

There is no question that his vocation was to keep alive the Shaker spirit in its purity and mediate that to the rest of us. I feel personally very much in debt to him for this. I realize more and more the vital importance of the Shaker "gift of simplicity" which is a true American charism: alas, not as fully appreciated as it should be. Ted was faithful to his call, and his work has born more fruit than we can estimate on this earth. His reward will surely be with those angelic ones whose work and life he understood and shared.

You are perhaps wondering what has become of the preface I was asked by him to write for *Religion in Wood*. I have been delayed, by a variety of tasks and chores. But the preface is now finished and needs only to be retyped. I will get it in the mail to you perhaps this week, perhaps later. But in any event I will be as quick about it as I can.

In the preface I have been bold enough to bring in quite a lot about William Blake. I hope you will not think this too venturesome, but I thought it would be worth while to write a preface that was an essay in its own right, and I hope it will add to the book. The text which Ted sent is very clear, interesting and even inspiring as was all that he wrote. I am most eager to see the new material in the illustrations.

With cordial good wishes and friendship,

Yours in Christ.

THOMAS MERTON TO
FAITH ANDREWS

July 23, 1964

Dear Mrs Andrews:

Here is the copy of the preface that I promised you the other day. I hope you will find it satisfactory. If I seem to be grinding my axe too hard in some places, we can always make a few changes. I am at your disposition.

With my very best wishes,

Cordially in Christ.

FAITH ANDREWS
TO THOMAS MERTON

August 18, 1964

Dear Thomas Merton,

Your most comforting letter—followed by the beautiful preface to our book—arrived almost a month ago. I have read them both every day and have not been conscious of the passage of time. Please forgive me.

Last month I spent a day in Cornwall, Conn. and had such a good time with Dorothy and Mark—mostly about what should happen to our Shaker library, some 75 museum pieces of furniture and the unpublished Mss (both books and articles) which Ted had completed—or nearly so.

You see the plan for Shaker Community Inc. where we worked so hard and with such faith—did not work out. After a year of legal hassle and great disappointment to Ted—we withdrew from the organization. However, the rare drawings and furnishings *delivered* there remain their property but the "undelivered" are in our name.

This is a brief resume in order for you to see what is happening and I would greatly appreciate any thoughts you might have as to the forwarding of Ted's work. The library, as you know is a very important one—the manuscript material, printed books and pamphlets and Ted's invaluable notes which accompany it. I want very much to make this library a memorial to Ted and have thought of Amherst College—since Ted was a graduate and felt close to it. Then, too, they are building the Robert Frost Memorial Library—even though Frost's collection was withdrawn by his daughter Leslie. It is my hope that wherever this library is housed that it will be a *unit*—since the Shakers represent a complete culture—I will furnish the room with appropriate study tables, prints, etc. It could be an extremely valuable tool for an "alive" American Studies Program.

Religion in Wood will soon go to the publishers—I am working on a sort of Memorial Book—the Shakers on occasion published such a book—although they were often bound in a drab and gloomy cover but contents very interesting. So many tributes have come in from all who knew Ted and/or his works—such as the one in your letter that I feel I should publish such a book and add it to the Shaker library.

Then, too, in our "legal" withdrawal from the Village, they agreed to publish a "Catalog of the Andrews Collection" now at Hancock. Ted's thought was that in the future—when the present personnel had left—it would be a record—one which would stand out from the many inferior additions. Ted had written the foreword—a beautiful essay—and completed the listing. I hope to have this ready next month. I am grateful for these occupations and pray for strength to complete at least some of them.

I will have your preface photo-stated before sending it off—so that I will not be without it.

The enclosed prayer may give you an idea of Ted's service—Shaker hymns—favorites of his—were also played and the beautiful recessional "I'll turn my face to Zion's Kingdom."

In deep gratitude always.

THOMAS MERTON TO
FAITH ANDREWS

October 30, 1964

Dear Faith Andrews:

It was good to get your letter last August and to know that the Preface was suitable. I am very glad you liked it. How is the book coming along? Who is going to publish it? I should be interested to hear, and I suppose that it will soon be ready. I would like very much to have three or four copies if possible.

I am very sorry to hear that there has been so much trouble about the collection. I wish I could help, but I have so little experience in these affairs and am so remote from the scene that I doubt if I could offer much advice that would make sense. I do think it would be important to have the collection all in one place. Amherst sounds like a logical selection. I hope that everything will work out.

By all means feel free to use anything I have said in the "Memorial Book" or anything else that will help point up the significance of Ted's work. Time will certainly show its spiritual importance. The Shakers were really an authentic form of American monasticism, and their fruits were and are a permanent witness to the reality of their experience. I think of them, and Ted and you, often. Do please keep me in mind when anything new is printed or said.

I am putting a couple of recent things of mine in an envelope: they may be of interest.

Do carry on with Ted's work. And may your efforts be blessed and fruitful.

Cordial good wishes always, in the Lord.

[PS] A letter of mine to Ted will be in my new book, which includes a section of letters.

FAITH ANDREWS
TO THOMAS MERTON

December 7, 1964

Dear Thomas Merton,

Thank you for your letter of October 30. Dover Publications who have put out three of our books very successfully in paperback, had agreed to publish the second furniture book—*Religion in Wood*. At a luncheon meeting with their president, Hayward Cirker, in Nov. 1963 plans were completed. Their contract department failed to send on an agreement and letters to Dover as to when we might expect the contract went unanswered. Early in July of this year I sent Cirker a wire asking when I might expect the contract and he replied apologetically that the department had been swamped with work but that I would hear very soon. However, I have not heard.

You may have heard that Doubleday requested a look at the Ms. and Ted and I had a talk with one of the editors—T. O'Conor Sloane III and left the Ms. with him. They turned it down on the basis that their salesmen thought it would have limited appeal. Interestedly enough, the two paper back editions have sold way over 10,000 copies.

A little over two weeks ago I had a request from the Indiana University Press and sent the Ms. on to them. They are interested, as you know, in communitarianism and have recently published a study of New Harmony—*The Angel and the Serpent*.

Last week I had a conference in Amherst with Prof. Henry Steele Commager—formerly of Columbia—re completion of the final three chapters of the book under contract to Syracuse University—*Hands to Work and Hearts to God—An Economic History of the Shakers.* His advice was that I go over Ted's notes on these chapters and make a rough draft of what I considered the "vital points." This I can and plan to do. A young friend of ours in American History—a student of the Mormons—is willing to undertake with me the completion of these chapters. This is a very difficult decision for me to make, since Ted's interests in the Shakers were so broad—his aesthetic summing up was so acute that unless a person has somewhere an artistic sense the light and truth just doesn't come through. Again it is "the gift to be simple." There is no room for self.

Professor Commager further suggested that on the remaining major book Mss to be published that I consider putting them into the hands of an agent. He recommended the Sterling Lord Agency in New York and wrote them a letter while I was with him. These are:

Visions of the Heavenly Sphere. A Study in Shaker Religious Art. 20 illustrations.

Come Life, Shaker Life. Two Hundred Shaker Songs.

There are some fifteen completed articles which I feel I can process. The one on "Sheeler and the Shakers" will appear in the Feb. issue of *Art in America.*

All signs now point to the Shaker library going to Amherst College. Commager is part of the American Studies Program and the library has much to offer in this field. It is hoped that the Robert Frost Memorial Library will be completed by Sept. 1965 so that I have plenty of time to put things together.

I am most grateful for your enclosures and read them many times—also shared them with one or two friends. The enclosed clipping from the *Amherst Alumni Quarterly* (fall issue) was written by a high school friend of Ted's and a colleague of his at Amherst. You doubtless know of Scott through his long friendship with Mark Van Doren and his setting up of the 100 great books program at St. John's.*

Please know that I gain such strength from your prayers and good wishes.

Gratefully yours.

PS The lovely 1965 Trappist calendar is on my desk awaiting the New Year.

I am eagerly awaiting publication of your new book in Jan.

---

*Scott Buchanan was involved with the setting up of the Great Books Program, in 1937 at St. John's College in Annapolis and contributed an obituary of Edward Deming Andrews to the *Amherst Alumni Quarterly*.

THOMAS MERTON TO
FAITH ANDREWS

April 20, 1965

Dear Faith:

I think often of you and of the book. Is it being published? I wonder if there is still anything I can do. This book *must* be published, it is so important.

Best Easter wishes,
Cordially in Christ.

A MEETING OF ANGELS

THOMAS MERTON'S PHOTOGRAPHS OF THE SHAKER VILLAGE OF PLEASANT HILL

1. COOPER'S SHOP, FROM EAST

2. FRONT (SOUTH) ELEVATION OF COOPER'S SHOP
AND WEST ELEVATION OF EAST FAMILY WASH HOUSE

3. WEST ELEVATION OF COOPER'S SHOP
AND REAR OF EAST FAMILY WASH HOUSE TO LEFT

4. WEST ELEVATION OF EAST FAMILY SISTERS' SHOP

5. EAST ELEVATION OF CENTRE FAMILY DWELLING

6. WEST ELEVATION OF EAST FAMILY WASH HOUSE

7. LOOKING SOUTHWEST, LEFT TO RIGHT: MINISTRY'S WORK SHOP,
MEETING HOUSE, CENTRE FAMILY DWELLING

8. EAST FAMILY BREATHREN'S SHOP
AND FRONT CORNER OF EAST FAMILY DWELLING

9. FRONT (SOUTH) EAST FAMILY WASH HOUSE,
AND CORNER OF REAR OF EAST FAMILY DWELLING

10. WATER HOUSE AND BREATHREN'S BATH HOUSE
AT CENTRE FAMILY AREA

II. FARM DEACON'S SHOP (WEST ELEVATION) WHICH WAS THE
FIRST PERMANENT CENTRE FAMILY DWELLING (1809)

12. FRONT (SOUTH) EAST FAMILY BRETHREN'S SHOP
WITH COOPER'S SHOP AT REAR

13. FRONT (SOUTH) EAST FAMILY DWELLING

14. EAST FRONT OF EAST FAMILY WASH HOUSE WITH
STONE GARDEN HOUSE AT THE NORTH LOT FAR IN THE DISTANCE

15. FRONT (SOUTH) OF EAST FAMILY DWELLING

16. LEFT TO RIGHT: EAST ELEVATION OF CENTRE FAMILY DWELLING,
WATER HOUSE, BRETHREN'S BATH HOUSE,
EAST FAMILY BRETHREN'S SHOP

17. EAST FAMILY BRETHREN'S SHOP WITH FRAME ELL
THAT WAS REMOVED DURING RESTORATION

18. WEST ELEVATION OF CENTRE FAMILY DWELLING,
THE LITTLE FRAME MINISTRY'S DINING ROOM AT REAR IS IN RUINS

19. COOPER'S SHOP FROM SOUTHEAST

20. INTERIOR, CENTRE FAMILY DWELLING

21. INTERIOR. CENTRE FAMILY DWELLING

22. CENTRE FAMILY DWELLING INTERIOR SHOWING 'ARCH'
OR COOKING FURNACE IN MAIN KITCHEN

23. CENTRE FAMILY DWELLING INTERIOR, EARLY EXHIBIT

24. CENTRE FAMILY INTERIOR, EARLY EXHIBIT
OF GARDEN SEED INDUSTRY

25. CENTRE FAMILY INTERIOR, EARLY EXHIBIT

26. CENTRE FAMILY INTERIOR

27. WEST ELEVATION OF TRUSTEES' OFFICE

28. WEST ELEVATION, EAST FAMILY DWELLING

29. WEST ELEVATION REAR OF EAST FAMILY DWELLING

30. WEST ELEVATION, EAST FAMILY SISTERS' SHOP

31. TRUSTEES' OFFICE

32. CENTRE FAMILY DWELLING EAST SIDE DOOR

ABOUT THE PHOTOGRAPHS

Thomas Merton visited Pleasant Hill on at least five occasions, and the photographs reproduced here were taken during at least two of those visits, though since the photographs were not dated some surmises must be made as to the visits on which they were taken.

Merton's first visit was in June 1959 and again on December 22nd 1959. At the time of these visits, however, Merton was not yet taking photographs.

He next visited on the 12th of January 1962. He certainly took photographs on this visit, and the winter scenes were almost certainly taken then. As he noted in his letter to Edward Deming Andrews on September 20th of that year, these are the photographs taken before any of the restoration had begun at Pleasant Hill. They are thus an important record of the remnants of the village as Merton first encountered them.

He returned again in May 1965, shortly after the conclusion of his correspondence with Faith Andrews. The photograph of Merton at Pleasant Hill was taken on this occasion by his friend and publisher James Laughlin of New Directions. The balance of the photographs, and certainly those that show the early exhibits reproducing the lives of the Shakers, appear to have been made during this visit.

Although he made one last visit in April 1968, he recorded that it was "pelting" with rain on this occasion, so it was unlikely that he took any photographs and, in any case, none of Merton's photographs show such conditions.

Though Merton never himself completed a photographic essay on Pleasant Hill, the images collected here are proof that the physical record of the Shaker's works affected his eye as much as their lives affected his heart.

P. M. P.

MERTON ON SHAKERTOWN

Marvelous, silent, vast spaces around the old buildings. Cold, pure light, and some grand trees... some marvelous subjects. How the blank side of a frame house can be so completely beautiful I cannot imagine. A completely miraculous achievement of forms.

The moments of eloquent silence and emptiness in Shakertown stayed with me more than anything else—like a vision.

Thomas Merton, *Turning Toward the World: The Pivotal Years,*
ed. Victor A. Kramer (San Francisco: HarperCollins, 1996), 194.

Pleasant Hill...always impresses me with awe and creates in me a sense of quiet joy. I love those old buildings and I love the way the road swings up to them. They stand there in an inexpressible dignity, simplicity, and peace under the big trees.

Thomas Merton, *A Vow of Conversation, Journals 1964-1965,* ed. Naomi Burton Stone (New York: Farrar Straus Giroux, 1988), 188.

The empty fields, the big trees—how I would love to explore those houses and listen to the silence. In spite of the general decay and despair there is joy there still and simplicity.

—Thomas Merton, *A Search for Solitude: Pursuing the Monk's True Life,* ed. Lawrence S. Cunningham (San Francisco: HarperCollins, 1996), 362.

I cannot help seeing Shakertown in a very special light, that of my own vocation. There is a lot of Shakertown in Gethsemani. The two contemporary communities had much in common, were born of the same Spirit. If Shakertown had survived it would probably have evolved much as we have evolved. The prim ladies in their bonnets would have been driving tractors, and the sour gents would have advertised their bread and cheese. And all would have struggled mightily with guilt.

Thomas Merton, *A Search for Solitude,* 287.

A MEETING OF ANGELS

APPENDIX

SHAKER FURNITURE

BY ANANDA K. COOMARASWAMY

Thomas Merton discovered Ananda K. Coomaraswamy's *The Transformation of Nature in Art* when he was working on his Master's dissertation on William Blake at Columbia University in the thirties. Years later he corresponded with Coomaraswamy's widow, Dona Luisa. In one letter Merton wrote that he saw in Coomaraswamy a model for spiritual unity "who has thoroughly and completely united in himself the spiritual tradition and attitudes of the Orient and of the Christian West."*

Merton and Ananda K. Coomaraswamy shared a number of friends in common, including the artist Victor Hammer and the Shaker scholars Edward Deming Andrews and Faith Andrews. The following review by Coomaraswamy of *Shaker Furniture* touches on many of the themes expressed by Merton in his correspondence with Edward Deming Andrews.

P.M.P.

---

*Thomas Merton, *The Hidden Ground of Love,* 126

Shaker Furniture* emphasizes the spiritual significance of perfect craftsmanship and, as the author remarks, "the relationship between a way of life and a way of work invests the present study with special interest." And truly a humane interest, since here the way of life and way of work (*karma yoga* of the *Bhagavad Gītā*) are one and the same way; and as the *Bhagavad Gītā* likewise tells us in the same connection, "Man attains perfection by the intensity of his devotion to his own proper task," working, that is to say, not for himself or for his own glory, but only "for the good of the work to be done." "It is enough," as Marcus Aurelius says (VI.2), "to get the work done well." The Shaker way of life was one of order; an order or rule that may be compared to that of a monastic community. At the same time, "the idea of worship in work was at once a doctrine and a daily discipline…. The ideal was variously expressed that secular achievements should be as 'free from error' as conduct, that manual labour was a type of religious ritual, that godliness should illuminate life at every point."

In this they were better Christians than many others. All tradition

---

*Edward Deming Andrews and Faith Andrews, *Shaker Furniture, The Craftsmanship of an American Communal Sect* (New Haven, 1937). Cf. Edward Deming Andrews, *The Gift To Be Simple: Songs, Dances and Rituals of the American Shakers* (New York, 1940).

has seen in the Master Craftsman of the Universe the exemplar of the human artist or "maker by art," and we are told to be "perfect, *even as* your Father in heaven is perfect." That the Shakers were doctrinally Perfectionists is the final explanation of the perfection of Shaker workmanship; or, as we might have said, of its "beauty." We say "beauty," despite the fact that the Shakers scorned the word in its worldly and luxurious applications, for it is a matter of bare fact that they who ruled that "beadings, mouldings, and cornices, which are merely for fancy, may not be made by Believers" were consistently better carpenters than are to be found in the world of unbelievers. In the light of mediaeval theory we cannot wonder at this; for in the perfection, order, and illumination which were made the proof of the good life we recognize precisely those qualities (*integritas sive perfectio, consonantia, claritas**) which are for St. Thomas the "requisites of beauty" in things made by art. "The result was the elevation of hitherto uninspired, provincial joiners to the position of fine craftsmen, actuated by worthy traditions and a guildlike pride.... The peculiar correspondence between Shaker culture and Shaker artisanship should be seen as the result of the penetration of the spirit into all secular activity. Current in the United Society was the proverb: 'Every force evolves a form.' ...The eventual result of this penetration of religion into the workshop, as we have noted, was the discarding of all values in design which attach to surface decoration in favor of the values inherent in form, in the harmonious relationship of parts, and the perfected unity of form."

Shaker art is, in fact, far more closely related to the perfection and severity of primitive and "savage" art (of which the Shakers probably knew nothing and which they would not have "understood") than are the "many shrewdly reticent modern creations"

---

*right proportion or perfection, harmony, radiance

in which the outward aspects of primitive and functional art are consciously imitated. Shaker art was not in any sense a "crafty" or "mission style," deliberately "rustic," but one of the greatest refinement, that achieved "an effect of subdued elegance, even of delicacy...at once precise and differentiated." One thing that made this possible was the fact that given the context in which the furniture was to be used, "the joiners were not forced to anticipate carelessness and abuse."

The style of Shaker furniture, like that of their costume, was impersonal; it was, indeed, one of the "millennial laws" that "No one should write or print his name on any article of manufacture, that others may hereafter know the work of his hands." And this Shaker style was almost uniform from beginning to end; it is a collective, and not an individualistic expression. Originality and invention appear, not as a sequence of fashions or as an "aesthetic" phenomenon, but whenever there were new *uses* to be served; the Shaker system coincided with and did not resist "the historic transference of occupations from the home to the shop or small factory; and new industries were conducted on a scale requiring laborsaving devices and progressive methods. The versatility of the Shaker workmen is well illustrated by the countless tools invented for unprecedented techniques."

We cannot refrain from observing how closely the Shaker position corresponds to the mediaeval Christian in this matter of art. The founders of the Shaker order can hardly have read St. Thomas, yet it might have been one of themselves that had said that if ornament (*decor*) is made the chief end of a work, it is mortal sin, but if a secondary cause may be either quite in order or merely a venial fault; and that the artist is responsible as a man for whatever he undertakes to make, as well as responsible as an artist for making to the best of his ability (*Sum. Theol.* ii-ii.167.2c and ii-ii.169.2 *ad* 4): or that "Everything is said to be good insofar as it is perfect, for in that way only is it desirable…. The perfections of all things are so many similitudes of the divine being" (*ibid.* 1.5.5c, 1.6.1 *ad* 2)—"all things," of course, including even brooms and hoes and other "useful articles" made *secundum rectam rationem artis.** The Shaker would have understood immediately what to the modern aesthetician seems obscure, Bonaventura's "light of a mechanical art."

It would, indeed, be perfectly possible to outline a Shaker theory of beauty in complete agreement with what we have often called the "normal view of art." We find, for example (pp. 20-21, 61-63), in Shaker writings that "God is the great artist or master-builder;" that only when all the parts of a house or a machine have been perfectly *ordered*, "then the beauty of the machinery and the wisdom of the artist are apparent;" that "order is the creation of beauty. It is heaven's first law [cf, Gk. κόσμος, Skr. *rta*]‡ and the protection of souls…. Beauty rests on utility;" and conversely, that "the falling away from any spiritual epoch has been marked by the ascendency of the aesthetics [*sic*]." Most remarkable is the statement that that beauty is best which is "peculiar to the flower, or generative period" and not that "which belongs to the ripened fruit and grain." Nor is the matter without an economic bearing. We treat "art" as a luxury, which the common man can hardly afford, and as something to be found in a museum rather than a home or business office: yet although Shaker furniture is of museum quality, "the New Lebanon trustees reported that the actual cost of furnishing one of our dwellings for the comfortable accommodations of 60 or 70 inmates would fall far short of the sum often expended in furnishing some single parlors in the cities of New York and Albany." One is moved to ask whether our own "high standard of

---

*according to the correct understanding of art

‡ κόσμος in Greek and *rta* in Sanskrit both refer to order in the universe

living" is really more than a high standard of paying, and whether any of us are really getting our money's worth. In the case of furniture, for example, we are certainly paying much more for things of inferior quality.

In all this there would appear to be something that has been overlooked by our modern culturalists who are engaged in the teaching of art and of art appreciation, and by our exponents of the doctrine of art as self-expression, in any case as an expression of emotions, or "feelings." The primary challenge put by this splendid book, a perfect example of expertise in the field of art history, may be stated in the form of a question: Is not the "mystic," after all, the only really "practical" man?

Our authors remark that "as compromises were made with principle, the crafts inevitably deteriorated." In spite of their awareness of this, the authors envisage the possibility of a "revival" of Shaker style: the furniture "can be produced again, never as the inevitable expression of time and circumstance, yet still as something to satisfy the mind which is surfeited with over-ornamentation and mere display," produced—shall we say at Grand Rapids?—for "people with limited means but educated taste...who will seek a union of practical convenience and quiet charm." In other words, a new outlet is to be provided for the bourgeois fantasy of "cult"-ure when other period furnitures have lost their "charm." The museums will undoubtedly be eager to assist the interior decorator. It does not seem to occur to anyone that things are only beautiful in the environment for which they were designed, or as the Shaker expressed it, when "adapted to condition" (p. 62). Shaker style was not a "fashion" determined by "taste," but a creative activity "adapted to condition."

Innumerable cultures, some of which we have destroyed, have been higher than our own: still, we do not rise to the level of Greek humanity by building imitation Parthenons, nor to that of the Middle Ages by living in pseudo-Gothic châteaux. To imitate Shaker furniture would be no proof of a creative virtue in ourselves: their austerity, imitated for our convenience, economic or aesthetic, becomes a luxury in us: their avoidance of ornament an interior "decoration" for us. We should rather say of the Shaker style *requiescat in pace** than attempt to copy it. It is a frank confession of insignificance to resign oneself to the merely servile activity of reproduction; all archaism is the proof of a deficiency. In "reproduction" nothing but the accidental appearance of a living culture can be evoked. If we were now such as the Shaker was, an art of our own, "adapted to condition," would be indeed essentially like, but assuredly accidentally unlike Shaker art. Unfortunately, we do not desire to be such as the Shaker was; we do not propose to "work as though we had a thousand years to live, and as though we were to die tomorrow" (p. 12). Just as we desire peace but not the things that make for peace, so we desire art but not the things that make for art. We put the cart before the horse. *Il pittore pinge se stesso;*‡ we have the art that we deserve. If the sight of it puts us to shame, it is with ourselves that the re-formation must begin. A drastic transvaluation of accepted values is required. With the re-formation of man, the arts of peace will take care of themselves.

---

*rest in peace

‡the painter paints himself

This book has been designed and typeset

by Jonathan Greene using Monotype Dante

for the text and Monotype Bell for display.

Printing and binding by Thomson-Shore.